Ship of Theseus

by

Christopher Willard

Ship of Theseus

Poems ©2016 by Christopher Willard
cwillard@telus.net
all rights reserved by the author

Cover photo by Steven B. Smith
agentofchaos.com / walkingthinice.com

Crisis Chronicles #82
ISBN: 978-1-940996-35-6
1st edition, 2nd printing

Published 31 March 2016
Crisis Chronicles Press
John Burroughs, editor
3431 George Avenue
Parma, Ohio 44134

crisischronicles.com
ccpress.blogspot.com
facebook.com/crisischroniclespress

I have been memorizing the internet
in order to say all that has been said.

I have tugged ropes tinged with kitten spittle.
I have put it in order.

This is what I mean:
Part 1.
Part 2.
Part 3.
Part 4. This is the longest, as usual.

Q. What becomes a constantly self-replacing system?
A. Although I know those who succumbed.

Q. If too many cooks spoil the soup?
A. Why then is Wikipedia so decent?

My dream was this: A splay-toothed girl named April
tapping out the contents of Pixy Stix
under the sap green glow of lilac bushes.

I lie on deck of the leaky ship and all is hope, I hope.
I steer by the correspondence of dim lights.

On campus a student came up to me and asked,
Where is the English building? I drew her a map to Parliament.

I provide names for belaying pins:
Amelia, Delilah, June-Betty, Afroza

as a peg-legged man climbs a ratline
up to where the clouds stiffen.

A man in a lit booth was always there
waiting for payment. That booth was so bright.

5

Let it be said that we can spin
more than has ever been spun.
Let us say that we can haul anchor.
Let us create tales.

The best of them are so little and covered with dust.

When they find life on Mars it will be
a banana peel laying on top of a flattened hat
embroidered with, *don't_be_a_topper.com*

a simple alien gesture, a once-thumbing nose-thumbing at our
    longevity.
In the quadrangle below my window, caterers
are dragging large black garbage bins.

They have fenced in the grass and soon
there will be a party. There will be little use for polarities.
Bubbly will flow through exposed teeth in tilted heads.

A Sikh security guard closes the gate. Inside the fence
is a pond where five mallard ducks dabble in umber water
and it could be suggested that any claim requires evidence

which is a different question than, *Is it true?*

Q. E-Ratio?
A. It was either an epithalamium or
something about an ostrich and a locket.

I lost my pen on the way to church and
was forced to do penance.

When the tongue stinks like Twinkies and Miller Lite,
don't eat peas. Sorry, I misspelled popcorn.

The larger the purse,
the closer the purse.

Upon ripped water-sod, upon rolling plains of water,
I plucked single drops of longing and I summoned eternity.

Think: A doily, a matchstick, and a spool. We flexed in teal pools
wishing, wishing, watching water run down our abs.

Q. Although confused?
A. Going a distance is not going the distance.

To compensate we say in unison, *Love was a stretch.*

The boys sang shanties at night:

Jugs of milk
hardtack bread
swig of grog
brain of dead

Oh, they were chastised in the best way.
Foul-mouthed frenzied dogs. Once in New Orleans,

a whore removed her teeth and turned on the drum machine.
I was ready to get dirty but not ready to get down

because I'd been warned: *Don't stick your hips toward the barn*
else the flies will come, boys will come, pigs will lie

with four feet in the air. Grandmother talked of needles
thrown into sunshine, and we were speckled and pricked.

10:26   The static at least.

10:27 Ruts bigger than a man's mind.
10:28 A mother sobs over her dead.
10:29 We hold our pain in the farthest corners of our lips.
10:30 Every night a new one.
10:31 We make apologies in four syllables.
10:32 I think I should.
10:33 Limp does not go far.
10:34 Q. When spring? A. When duck.
10:35 That would mean not writing this down.
10:36 My minute:
10:37 This goes on.
10:38 And off.
10:39 I almost didn't look.
10:40 Imagine what we will say.
10:41 Echoes and demands.
10:42 The goal is to pose and to do it relatively well.
10:43 When rust becomes a privilege.
10:44 Dust in the big way.
10:45 It became inappropriate.
10:46 The rapture of one, or fewer.
10:47 Peering into icicles.
10:48 Dreams of rattling pebbles.

I'm my own little coroner, in my own rubber room:
Another tar song to peel the shellac off a beetle's back.

I called them on deck. I boomed,
Relative absurdity remains relative absurdity.
Let's talk over tacos.

Grandmother was a hex nut, fashioning silence with
an old evil eye. She sported glass shards for earrings. She sang,

When the dogwoods are peeling their bark,
yer mother will still be milking.

She wrecked her brain on the information highway.

No really, I did, I caught an atom in a glass
and covered it with my hand to keep it in there.

Q. What had slipped?
A. Certainly not the security of repetition.

She blamed aging upon gravity, same as scientists.
She saw the future and it was all wrinkles and health issues.

Q. How does it fail miserably?
A. How does it succeed fabulously?

A guy in a movie had what we would call a gigantic foot
and he stole a front-loader in broad daylight.

Q. Where was he going to hide such a thing?
A. Under a peanut shell?

We see the storm arising. We perceive edges on the waves.
We are gonna crash. We are gonna eat clocks on the green.

*Red fir at night,
squirrels take delight.*

They sang to relieve the stress.
They debated lopping even more fingers.

*My name is Trashy Trailer
and at life I am a failure
which is why my pics are posted
upside down.*

And all across the internet, in the broadest sense –

which reminds me of the funny story about the Bulgarian
    optometrist.

Q. The sign says *Teach Abroad.*
A. Which broad?

When it rains,
although it rains,
when the rust drops from the iron basket,
when the studdingsails flap
cats yowl and the cordage shakes with the echoes of cat yowls.

It's not the persuasion
that will turn the tide of eyes
but the insidious lip-sticking.

Before this, paintings done by that famous artist: Gerthird Reichter,
Son of Fog Bo with hideousness of sphincter.

Q. Isn't a moron just more off than on?
A. Say it ain't slo-mo.

And then came the screaming hypnotism.

I'm out for a breath of flesh air
which is better than a kick in the clam.

Touched by a realtor.
What a chunk of luck.

The blanket smelled of rancid sweat
the bedbugs were on fire.
The girlfriend's **** was sopping wet
the boyfriend's **** rose higher.

Seriously, is this the wrong side of everything?

Why didn't God, in his infinite power, make a second world
right next to the first so he could say, *Here ya go,
see? This is what you could have been.*

A cat named Meteor and a kitten named Lickin' Little
lay next to a petrified rosebud. My cabin was dark
but I knew them from the shine of their eyes.

Alienus ex machina, but what was their intention?

Near the Isle Nuku'alofa of I was fisted by an alien,
under the glow of St. Elmo,
but don't tell my mother – she'll be jealous.

Q. It appears there are those among us who are true and good.
A. We will have to do something about them.

It appears the same-old still holds significance for some:
relationships, jobs, the continual sorting of the redescribed.

A certain straightforwardness appeared upon her face,
which I called preservation, and this alone
caused me to pick up the books: *Tom Sorry,
Huckleberry and Dingleberry*. The past is over
and we move through as though untroubled.

She collected the errors, she edited; these became
the mistakes of her life.

It distressed the aliens to see her in this state of inefficiency.

Time to grow-op and sell out.

We must reflect. We must recollect.
Morality brings consequences. Art as a presequence event.

Near Tongataboo Harbour, we separated into two piles
the skulls of the slain.

I am Dr. Vonk
and I know this little songk
Kann heit, kein might
first **** I lick tonight.

I always sing, *butterflies are free*
as I visit the natural history museum
to observe them pinned in their cases.

So the aliens come and they want to play Twister.
We do too.

But the aliens have more appendages than we do,
and so they keep winning.

We refuse to play anymore and call them little green cheaters.

They retaliate with massive F5 tornadoes.
We again invite them to play but this time on Damien Hirst spot
    paintings
laid across Kansas, and this causes the aliens to break apart.
They are so desperate to win.

The squall hit like a fart in a funnel.
It was downright know-nothingness multiplied.

Their eyes filled with water, when the rains came,
when they looked up,
when the water fell,
when the fields filled,

and when some suggested even the sex was better.

Poor little weedwacker never bothered any one.

I prefer my dick as I prefer my science, hard.
I sleep uncringing. I believe in the rationality of my speculations.

I am the head that dropped into the basket
and this is my story:

We pepper sprayed the mountain goats because
we had spent a lot of money putting the window in the wall
and they were spoiling the view.
Later we fed the goats wintergreen to make up.
Later we discovered our reasons were bad ballast.

It is over when:
the butterfly kerthumps,
the monkey swings are inert,
when the porridge cools.

I will have a hopeful drink and I will pursue reason.
When did our search for truth mean we started telling the truth?

Poem comprised of first words from page 3
of Geoffrey Gorham's *Philosophy of Science*:

geometry,
scientific tool
astronomers
natural
supernatural
The Apollo)
radically little
sixth Miletus
ambitious forces held
underlying water,
liquid the

our eyeballs.
reductionist,
ing earth, *nous,*
aim
which world
crashing models,
accounting natural and
The geometry.

Higher levels of art only know customers.

*With ink-stained teeth
and tits of glass.*

Iamb pentameter but so are you says I.
Get some shut-eye before the walleye.

Q. Do I know you?
A. No, but you will.

I dig my own hole.

A styrofoam cup remains, today, tomorrow,
this is a problem when the dining room has no lights.

Q. That umbrella of 60-watts?
A. Oh.

Shine on silver, shine one more for me.

One stream, two channels.
I send messages to verify my ability to receive.

So I ran to my post on the prow but you already knew that.
I sang, *There were things in the crib, things in the crib* –
which reminded me of a funny story of Macbeth's burping.

An idiot's minister is also everybody's minister.

So I played a drinking game with myself
again, as usual,
and I won again, as usual,
and I lost again, as usual.

I don't think *Stick it to the Man*
was ever a gay pride parade slogan.

Hark. All the worldly waves slide at the same rate.

I was a lubricator and a fussbudget
selling dummies on the side, a nickel a pop,
leaning forward, hanged in chains once caught.

In New Orleans, I said, *You may have won the bottle
but I won the whore.*

My compendium of useless things
grows larger as I grow older.
It now includes porcelain fungus,
not that I want it that way.

The stains grow bigger too, and I imagine
a frequent shuttle to a distant place
where holes are a significant feature
and once-holes, now filled, sag unceremoniously.

I entertained them with movie after movie
each with a theme of transplanted hands:
murderer's hands, choking hands,
finger-giving hands. We knelt and gave thanks to Hobbes.

The shadow of my ship indicates something

of who I was, like a faulty analogy, or the cheap restoration
of a Chinese screen.

And there were:

Those who walked as though their life depended
Those who, although they hanged
Those who wobbled but who were not drunk
Those who gave advice with a syringe
Those who wore semi-transparent shorts and opaque panties
        of phthalocyanine
Those who required monthly visits
Those who desired
Those who knelt because they were weary
Those who sniffed too hard
Those who preferred patterns
Those who walked on their toes
Those who suffered weak epiglottises
Those who made books of lead
Those who polished pink aluminum, or planned to
Those who were jailed because their brother committed
        the crimes
Those who offered without being asked
Those who knew every single word
Those who plucked
Those who believed in punctuality
Those who cooked clams in small cans.

I was a latchkey lackey,
ambitious, attracted to salt-licks,
avoiding festivals on hot Sundays.

I keep my ear honed for the heir to the throne.
I punched as though I had eyes on my knuckles.

I sailed to the dock, docked the sail,

sold the ship, shipped the sail,
I had nothing left to do
but to shoot myself.

Q. And the good news?
A. I talked myself out of it.

Oh, they asked me who I was.
And I said,
and I said,
and they said, *What's your name now?*

I packed the prow with mongrels misfitted by a fragile god.
Snow falling on sinners:

The hobbled, the half-legged, the horse-eyed, with
wood and tin can prosthetics, they all joined the clatter,
a crew beneath a buffeted sail:

Pig Fermouth, Toodles McKitten, Art Libris, Tang the Tongue Twangler, Cruddy Udders, Dertie Tiffiender, Yardsticks Withdrawal, The Mouth that Bored, 7. Sinsat Wonce, A. Pickled E., Half Rotten Crudites, What Stunk Still Stinks, Farthing Hunter, The Nun's Unused Count, Stumble Drunk, Two Pegs for Ears, Potbellied Botfly, The Smear, Hound Putty, I Can Reach My Ears, Quatre Pates Patates, Farting Minister, Fifty Yard Lineyes, Code B689, Polyester Astroturf, Tortoisean Flippers, Dirty Molars, All the Ham at One Sitting, Sir Fluster Cluck, Honorable Suck-a-Pebble, Philadelphian Drool Cup, Tripe Sausage, Hoboken Belly Sweats, Loafer Hole, Arse Drippings, Finger MeGud, Gluten Tag, Three Wheeler Perch Dealer, Al Mostupright, What C. Chuckingup, One Fancy Leap, Fanny Coop, Copping A. Fist, Lou Lou Vermin, Constable Fudge, Whence Tot, Flushing Cuthbert,

Moulu's Maker, Divergent Deeds, Rubben Soul, Spinnaker's Paddlemaster, Limpy Lumptoe, Slumpy Dumpkins, The Crow's Bent Beak, Fashionista Alert, Calling All Porpoises, Jumblebean, Fat Futures and Thin Presences, Code for Badgers, One Web Joint, Anabolic Denial, Thud Sucker, Mortar Neck, Scared Sacred, The Undeniable, Scrum for One, Touch Scream, Monsieur Frottage Cheese, Dim Dimples, Foolhardy with Tobacco Chew, Nicklestore Teeth, Lips like Lugers, Rhyme Pump, Hose Without End, Touchall Lickall, Ne'er a Clean Table, Monkey's Pa, Tremor of Indent, Male Malapplied, Approaching Graffiti, Burgermeister Sgraffito, Neon Incognito, Dotted Line, Funicular Fred, On End and Again, Orthogonal Orbs, Ye Olde One Pointe, Scream of Concussion, Knit the Knotty Nitpicker, Back Garbage, Takes Two Seats, Frypan Face, Digits Forward, Shorty Prolong, It was Juicy, Cornered Cat and Tree'd Pussy, Arkansas' Illicit, Backhatward, Insomniac's Wet Dream, One Brickless, Hate Fall, Seignor Exculpatory, Bait Breath, Gum Veil, 46th Street Zircon, Howling Owlet, Tin for Dura, Carafe Lathe, Waxy Rim, Iron Pot of Bubbling Spandex, Flexy-ass, Belt Loop Victim, Slender Bowlegs, Old Man Riveter, The Skunk of Trinidad, Many Minipants, Cuffed Enough, With a Pencil All is Possible, Loins of Dim Lightning, Max Pecas, Jack and Gin, Tumbling Laughter, Beardrugger, Alley Squab, Bold Boy with Billiards, Butt Butt who's Got the Butt, Long Drawn Sparrow, Chiffon Gizzard, Captain Jeffy Pop, Bog in the Bread Basket, Edda Gobler, Charmed Macau, Capital F. from Odessa, Yacht Licker, Inky Tooly Braunleigh, Gordon Cromwelt, Rising Weave, Century City Pity, Meltdown Man, The Dongan Freak, Epaulottaluv, Slur Skin, The Morea Grifter, Once a Dime Always a Dime, Flip Coiner, Brazil Dazzler, Red Wheedleborrower, Opinion Den, Guano's Ferry, Private Sequined Blueberry, Hunchdork of Notre Gnome, Orff Dot, Vinyl Spider,

Eggs-a-Dozzing, 3 For 5 Euros, Bundle of Glands, End all Harmonicas, Foucault's Perineum, The Drink of Luxury, Aerial View, Midder Skuff, Earwax and Tear Ducts, Apes on Acid, A Lot of Crying San Francisco 49ers, Four Bananas But One Too Many, Noisette Doll, Chicago Candylapper, Once A. Pickaxe, Two Elbows Too Splayed, Velvet Fly, Spray on Shadow, Denim from Mars, Phone Poison, Burrs on a Fetter, Stinky Panty Band, Uncle Soiled Himself, Monocled Rebus, The Sao Paolo Slink, Jungle Beaten, I Saw It First, Yurt Squatter, One Fist Many Mouths, Squalor Moth, The Snakeskin Tree, Blunt Laser, A Dump and Leave, Whassup Beard, The White Patella, D.M.Z. Thomas, Squirting Bubbles, Mad Mexican, Swivel Hipster, First Act Revolver, Vlad the Intolerable, Poison Bleudang, Jowls, Miniature Donkey Lover, Weenie Widow Weekly, Too Sou Too Cher, Code of Mohammad Ali, Espace Vicodin, Change to Subjects, Stretching to India, No Exes, Gulag Wannabe, Death and Menace, Umeda Skittering Crawdaddy, Tzar Flexiglas, Wet Cheeked Wonder, I Floss with Broomstraws, First at the Window, Plopping Flesh, One Long Smoke, Hips Like Car Seats, Upagully Downagully, Detroit Debt Crisis, DJ Flunkafew, Yo Yo Pap, Dr. Brow, Lost His Breaks, Short Acre, Thick Bill, Barbarous Mitigator, The Yodeling Shaver, Widow's Theme, Calamitous John, Simulacra Murderer, Supersnail, Hardly Relevant, When the Tide Goes Out, Abandoned Mind, Lap of Leisurely, Mignon Mongol, Easy for You Touché, Swapmeet Galoot, Clipper, Preposition Eight, Ongoing Auditory Propagation, Ham Band, Solong Sarong, Itch Heisse, Yore Fault, Sewer Peep, Baited Faith, Slumptown's Dirty Angle, A Repugnant Pregnant, Flesh Dismissal, Shoes Flat No Hat, Medicine Doll, Gross Purse Alert, Fried Lichen, Upskirt Downboy, Schnozz Nozzler, Three Times Around, Claude Pebble, A. Symbol Plan, Non-touching Navels, Pour Emporter,

Kudasai Kudasai, Ripping Stitches, Communist Chunnel, Apple Cord, Too Deep To Dip, True Toads Converged, Snappy the Suspender, Funktown's Raccoon, Des Moins in the Mountains, Double E's Treble F's. Young One Foot, Snaky Very Snaky, Sleepy Sod, Hi Ho Hod, Flannigan's Wank, Fizzy Wink, Crwth the Tooth, Funny Aikens, Oxford's Pathos, Maud's Made Maid, Das Stiefel, Parent Theses, Parson Arson, What Floats, Paulmall Dude, Carts Aplenty, Hippomene's Crabs, Lazy Bus and Sleazy Lust, Mutable Erratic Warbler, Beautiful Erotic Gargler, Urn Urn, Nipple Splitter, Pimple Riot, Madame Pompadour's Burning Thorns, Batterfly, The Plunging Sissy Pig, Four Scars and Seven Beers Ago, Our Mutual Fiend, Squidlike Bubbies, Out of Service, Once a Dill Always a Dill, Bleck Breath, Whiffs of Clover, Shrill Like Light Telephones, Say Hello to Fog, He Who is Always Opposite, Mr. Thrope, High Hat and Low Dong, Uncarressed D, Such-a-Tongue, The Final Slant, Perky Yes Perky, Vladoko Nabomir, Three Half Past, Fleet Street's Yeti, Gnat Slipper, Wedgie Pudding, That Smarts, Turdy de Luxe, Tres des Guerres, Christian Marc, P.T. Ahole, Eh Eh Eh, Bay Haven's Firth, Part Moon's Bastard, Heat Rash, Rutger's Girl, If You Eat Too Many, The Uniform Travesty, New Noodle Done Old Style, Frisson with Bowtie, Dream Yawa, The Hot Smell of Pavement, Worm Dangler, Voltaires Uvula, TukTuk Wally, Floor Raised Doug, Señor Stile, F2 Gassboy, Athens Masher, Crois Baby, Minnimus, Toby Bar Tab of Brablewood, Pinneedle a Penny, Crow Cause, Croak Haws, Cree Hoss, Half-cent Dinner, Pinworm Willie, Wacky Quohog, Wagon Full of Giblets, Such Distant Screaming, Cumulus Dumbass, True Man Capote, Shitty Shitty Bung Bung, Staremister, Oogle Me Gonads, Withdraw McGraw, Splitting Damage, Slit Stink, Big Bellows Fellow, Mal de Teat, Ingrown Hangbrain, Fumble Fly, Sloppy Soliloquies, Poe's Muse, Nero's

Wart, Caesar's One Damn Dump, Lick Dixon, Died Root, Princess Dead, T. Portley, Furnbaugham the Cheese Roller, Dingingham's Dandy, Defective Vanity, A New Way to Say Nothing, Al Newalgia, Twitchingside, Oink Factor, Two Bees in a Bramble, Subcavernous Reeker, Punch Lime, Spit, Hepatitis B-minus, Almost Dare, The Vain Leper, Cool for Scoundrels, Tit Farmer, Swamp Bungler, 21 Gun Refute, Never Mint, Two Parts and a Fiddle, Any Sperm in a Port, The Village Vice, Daily Nuisance, Anteater's Lashing, Such Such Droppings, MacHaile Tvunshein, Scythe My Buddy Scythe, One Across One Down, So So Duke, Eight Knuckles for Nothing, Ah A. Cheese Cutter, Ewe Tester, Slam Ramp, Landed on It, Rubbed Soldiers, The Bouquet of Grunt, Marathon Moron, The Hobnobber of Flaunted Thighs, Presidential Pardon, Chamonbert Chamonbert, Carpet Bragger, Anti-bellum Bandicoot, Still-so-Still, Please Sheer May I, Stiletto on My Mind, Venus Army, Slappin' His Lapin, Freischule für Dummkopfs, Inch of Dirt, David's Fig Thief, Go Terry and Delouse, Premier Pyrex, Pudding Pants, Piss n' Bits, Cockaracca, Juan de Lust, Ne Hee Maury Lucrum, Rittenhauer's Mistress, 10th Street Avignon Goony, Stash, The Mule of Mountbatten, Eichmann's Little Ditty, Capuchin Ghoul, Blind Bobby's Attaché, Kobe Caryatid, Mock Picasso, Pecs-a-Million, Kancas City Freeloader, Fringe Squab, Sick Lily, Dago Lass, The Alluder, The Sow's Bungling, Two Pups of a Litter, Grazia Strip, Dad's Pud, Tyrolean Agony, Crime Against Creoles, The Livelier Liar, The Diplomatic Squeeze, Julio Homeopath, Human Jug Band, Doppelgangster, Nextdoor Noise, Cramp Stamp, The Beadle with Itchy Dominoes, Powder Bug of Philly, Laps up Puddles and More, Copulates Like Creamed Corn, The Damsel of Daintytown of Dampishire, He Who Treads in Half Circles, Crocodile Tears and Rhinoplasty, The Golden Bargeman with Collagen Balloons in his Overalls, Once a Lederhosen Lover Always a Lederhosen Lover, Vents at Both Ends Both Well Used, Veterinarian of Philosophy for an Ill Cur, Bedecker of Bondhill, Tourmaline My Lovely, Double O's Second, He Naps With Dangling Strings in Rusting Saabs, Latex Bath Caps R Me, Moulin Rough, Hen's Eggs-a-Plenty, Capistrano Caterwaulerer, Beowulf's Muddier Partner, Thor's Drum Dum Dum, Romanian Rutwrangler for Cheap, John Queere's Back Ho, Pretty Soon, Uncle's Lap Warmer, Sebastopol's Hand Me Around and Down, Boone's Canoe Spooner, Number 1 Digital Prick, Chat Poulet, Long Story Shot, Slit Clogger from the Emotive Side of Blowhole, Rhode Island Razor Burn, Another Corporate Monkeywhore, Convincing Himself of Everything Meaning Less, Riker's Screw and Rawhide Rascal, Pimento Addiction, Bear Toboggan, Somewhat Better than a Bicycle Seat, Partner Blender, Tots, Fun with Rash Cream, Nautilus Fartman, His Bung Undone, Don't Tell Mammy from Debtford Mews, Can't Shower Enuf, Drip McQueen, As he Mouths au Moins au Moins, Disembodied Head-san from Honshu District Eight, Hey Bobo That Ain't Toblerone, Buttledare and Shittlecock, Salted Ropeburns, Private Places in Public Spaces, Facial Hair Like a Poor Haiku, Nausea in Tightness, When Toby Went He Clutched the Sacred Vial, Kilkenny's Saccharine Killjoy, So Little So Loose, Solder Buoy, Barnwell's Slogan – 'It Never Fit in the First Place', Brunei Town's Sick Noose, Fistula Marauder, Bellowing Swanee River, Spoof Plumper, What the Dog Did and Shall Do Again, Waste Not Want, Chuck Boy's Chew Toy, Once Upon a Bedsheet Dirty, He Who Sits on a Seat But is it His Own?, Coffin Salad, Darning Quilts and Humping Bees, SASE Endorsed But Don't Use It, Bloodthirsty Reachdealer and Co., Sons of Blackhead and His Musty Minks, Womb of the Ungrown Groaner, Buck Teeth & Doe Teeth, Equals Organized Opposition, Wet

Stretcher, I'd Walk a Kilometer for a Long Thermometer, Punty's Rubber Oblong, Twaddle on a Nightingale, Waterproof Wool, Gerty's Hair Brownies Taste as Bad as They Smell, Major Hole, Deep Pain Trombonists, Put to the Test, Trifranqueshire Farmhand, Senile Weasle, You Call it Seduction We Call it Sandpaper, A Burning Confirmation, Grubby Conditioning and a Winesop Gnat, Mostly Gristle and Mohair, Micawber Dozes and Dreams of a Macramé Heart, Lincoln of Logtown, A Swiftian Crime, Sofa Stain, Detroit Narc's Benchmark, Stencil, Mongoloid Fizzfanatic, Blown Bills on a Seedy Street, Clichy's or St. Denis' Daredevil, No Tool Toolbox, Cobbler's Strudel, Our Creamy Greek Cousin, Bedlam's Foul Aide, Loins of Llondyn, Odorous and Unobtainable, Skirt Issue, Lacan A. Thrope, Mesta's Dropping Barometer, The Enormity of Ft. Lee, Evelyn Noir, Charlemagne's Umbrella Squad Leader, Upsydaisy, A Hot Wind Blowing Incessantly and Unnecessarily, Fongles Fongel, The Breach of the Vertical Maginot Line, The Smell of a Four Fingered Glove, The Smelting Conspiracy, Bi-bim-bap, May 1968-67, Oxpecker's Vomitorium, Too Permeable for Tomfoolery, Remedial Homo Sapiens Sapiens.

Chord's the word.
In the old days there were three.

I sold the ship, bored the hole,
made the cut, cut the plug,
plugged the hole, shipped the whole.

Our approach will be Teutonic. Our purpose is methodological.
Our club no longer accepts food vouchers in lieu of dues.

In New Amsterdam's harbor I recalled the taste of a toothpick under the tongue after a dodgy pierogi party at Veselka.

I scowled under what I thought was a crow's nest,
only to discover it was a widow's peak.

I entertained my crew with *The Miracle Worker*
and we watched it the way it was meant to be watched:
with the sound and picture off.

Sometimes I wonder about those who propose to know,
like it's a form of hives across the abdomen.

With a pushed up nose
and bunched up eyes
with a garden hose
between his thighs.

It is this sort of thing I continually find
myself apologizing for although it's not my doing.

Yet, through the curled and bubbly foam
my ship ploughs onward
in search of the Isle of Elusiveness.

She came into the world bawling.
She bawled through life.
She left the world bawling.

Q. No pain no gain, but what did she gain?
A. A surgeon's version of curdled reassurance.

To die within a Pomo paradigm – for what can life mean
when there is no meaning, if only interpretations exist?

Q. We asked that question at the start.
A. And we forgot to answer it.

So mama don't take my chromosome away.

The giant Spanish slugs have arrived.
They prowl the deck at noon
and a woman at dinner says she's seen one
eating a rabbit. She uses the word *gruesome*.

I sailed my ship like a seed upon a tongue.
I clipped my fingernails to withstand the doldrums and watched
the dark petrels fly perpendicularly away from the ship.

I installed a radar encoder.

I whipped a hundred or so dogs
as oarlocks strained on metal pins
in time to the dripping grease.

What nasty meant is not what nasty means.
From the boots down, that's where the steps begin.

On the earth, sits a metal plate which says,
Below this, a rod extends to the core of the earth.

All who lust
eventually rust.

Four bells now.

We edged Bowditch Island and I remembered the tip of a pinecone
and I realized my foibles and I was saddened.

I decided to go half-ahead for the view
although the blur remained. We were spinning
side-long, whistling wildly in wooly waters.

Sooner or later all water leads to Hell.

I do my best to remain above,
on bark with board ballast I have risen
on turn and tide drawn by engorged moons.

Kittens crawl out of coiled ropes
and look upon those moons
with what appears to be drunken wonderment.

The soles of my shoes are thick
and I query whether I can shun myself.

We furled the sails. We bleached the cabin boy
while he scrutinized with large watery lips. He can count to nine
for he is missing a finger.

In New Amsterdam I tossed a trail of cans from a hansom window
and I knew the way we entwined our arms spelled t-r-o-u-b-l-e.

My goal was to suck the color out of your eyes
inspired as I was by the white sky.

Q. The muse cajoles?
A. The captain commands.

Logbook. June 25.
Incidents: 5:27 pm. – An abandoned ship was
reported near Shore Cove. The sails were furled,
the binnacle locked.
9:08 pm. – A woman telegraphed from the
Land of Nod to say a man had taken her
wits and would not return them.
Logbook. June 27
Incidents: 7:19 am. – A yellow kitten was
seen sitting near the white whipstaff. We

have no animal refuge league.
2:48 pm. – A snotty responded to
a noise in the bilge. The door was found open
but the area was "pretty much condemned."
Logbook. June 28.
Incidents: 7:49 pm. – An unknown person(s)
scribed an obscenity on the escutcheon
below the ship's name.
Logbook. July 1.
Incidents: 9:09 pm. – A woman's voice was
heard saying that unless we returned home
immediately she was going to throw her
rabbit across the town line. A boy was put on
watch.

That gutter is the other gutter.

A story about the bobcat cubs rescued
made me happy until one was found to have a broken jaw
and I thought, *poor little bobcat cub.*

Gather ye round:
We who stand on two feet – stand on.
We who stand on two feet do so
because we don't have three feet.

Which reminded me of a story about a ditz
and a cunning microbiologist who dated for a time.

What it said on page 68, column 3 was
what it said on previous pages.

Seriously: Same as previous.

We put the block-press on the bench and promised to press.
Yes, my friends, the chair has lost its velveteen pallor.

I played an air on a catgut
with a bow that had lost its rosin
and it was siren song.

Between greasy fingers, I held a long hair from my beard
and I stood on the stern and he extended a once cracked arm,
the better to mark wind, and therefore, time.

When I had finished memorizing the internet
I looked around for something new to do.

It was the difference between placing the eye to the hole
and walking into a large storm drain.
But I sensed something visceral.

The possibilities seemed so stale.

Near Mele Bay I met a hitchhiker who had two thumbs on one hand,
and I asked him, *Why do you have two thumbs on one hand?*
He said, *One for the road.*

A man with no hope will polish a penny.
A word wrapped in brass. A black sail seen at night.
We stroked 170 oars.

It was such a logical step: unsuction the skull,
engage in a bit of rapid prototyping, and voila, a public procession.
Such a fine line between violence and artistic gesture.

When I unfogged the window, I noticed ducks on a patch of ice
out in the man-made pond and it was my impression
that they were making what altruists call a meaningful contribution

or a meaningful substitution, and then a surge of hookers
pounded along 14th Street chanting *Cap'n my Cap'n* and I

thought, here comes bad news bared.

Q. Riddled agenda?
A. Ridden agenda.

My mate took a fast bus out of a slow town.
The dirty tar. He sang, *I heard it through the rape vine
that soon yer gonna be mine,* etc, etc.

He got his due. He slammed his nuts into a railing.
His peers found this hilarious but his peer didn't.

And he, like the others, was graced with the cat o' nine
for his doggerel. He bled with ease.

Q. And what about those hard to remove stains?
A. Such as guilt and remorse?

On a crisp day, when icicles hung long from yardarms
you made me lose my love-flower,
and the icicles were blown sideways by the gale.

I was roflmao and you were huffing and puffing
and I felt the bouncing prow on the breast of waves.

A pirate will tell you, *ne'er a bad hair day.*
We were travellers, desperate maybe-men
with ugly brows and twigs for our teeth cleaning.

I now type with my tongue.

I got a gal in Louisiana. Guess her name? Louise or Anna?

Q. How to stop coughing, but with rules of civility?
A. This was difficult.

Gleason is the word, Gleason is the way.
And away we go. To the moon.

Kittens gawked. Kittens overpronated in admiration.

There was a handwritten title on a certain video,
but that was long ago when the aesthetics of stone blocks
were still appreciated.

Q. Why is there something rather than nothing?
A. Because the hog goddess inhales resin and cries on cue.

Peace is the word, peace is the way.
And onward.

My ship scales the surface. My ship causes this ocean to exist.
The mewing of my oak kitten lulls me still,
the spit of Caeneus is upon my nape, driving me forward.

What was once light has now fallen.

Q. What if you did it all again?
A. But this time slowly.

www.ingramcontent.com/pod-product-compliance
Lightning Source LLC
Chambersburg PA
CBHW071243090426
42736CB00014B/3208